Surviving Him

A True Story of Narcissistic Abuse, Legal Warfare, and a Mother's Relentless Fight for Her Children

By

Diana Levin

Table of Contents

Introduction 4
Chapter 1: The First Lie 6
Chapter 2: All Surface, No Soul 9
Chapter 3: Convenient Amnesia 13
Chapter 4: The Proposal That Meant Nothing 15
Chapter 5: The Biggest Mistake of My Life 18
Chapter 6: Back Where I Shouldn't Be 20
Chapter 7: The First Pregnancy 24
Chapter 8: Choosing to stay 28
Chapter 9: The Erosion 31
Chapter 10: A Child Without a Home 36
Chapter 11: The Trap 42
Chapter 12: No Way Out 46
Chapter 13: The Final Fall 58
Chapter 14: The Edge and the Climb 63
Chapter 15: When Power Slips 68
Chapter 16: When Control Fails, Chaos Begins ... 73
Chapter 17: The Breaking Point 75
Chapter 18: $300,000 and a Shrug 79
Chapter 19: Court-Approved Character Assassination 82
Chapter 20: The Line I Wouldn't Cross Again 90
Chapter 21: When He Took Aim at Her Too 92
Chapter 22: The Price of Doing the Right Thing ... 95
Chapter 23: The Day I Became the Monster in Her Eyes 98

Chapter 24: The Relapse 100
Chapter 25: The Goodbye I Never Wanted to Say
.... 101
Chapter 26: The Ones Who Should Have Helped
.... 103
Chapter 27: The Moment She Saw Him 105
Chapter 28: Let Him Come 108

Introduction

This isn't a guide. It's not a list of tips or rules. You won't find the usual breakdowns of gaslighting, gray rock, or no-contact here, at least not in the clinical way you've probably already seen a hundred times.

This is a true story.

A real, lived experience of narcissistic abuse that spanned decades, not months. Not a few red flags and a clean break. This is what it looks like when you're caught in the storm for years, when the manipulation is subtle enough to confuse you, brutal enough to destroy you, and strategic enough to make everyone else think you're the problem.

I wrote this because when I was in it—deep in it—all I found were dry definitions, bullet-point advice, and hollow encouragement that barely scratched the surface of what I was going through.

What I needed back then was someone who had *been there*.
Someone who knew how it felt when your reality was twisted beyond recognition. When your children were weaponized against you. When the court system, the social workers, and the people who were supposed to help didn't.

I wrote this because I never found a full story. A *real* one.
Start to finish. No sugarcoating. No vague examples. Just the truth. Ugly, painful, liberating truth.

If you're here, maybe you're still inside the fog. Maybe you've just begun to wake up to what's happening. Maybe you're already out, but still carrying the scars. Wherever you are in it, I hope this book helps you recognize the patterns faster than I did. I hope it gives you the strength to walk away sooner than I could. And I hope it reminds you that you're not crazy, you're not alone, and you're not powerless.

This is what it looks like to survive him.
And this is me, surviving.

Chapter 1: The First Lie

I came from a broken home, a single child who never truly knew what love felt like. The moment I turned eighteen, I left, searching for something more—something that would fill the void of never feeling truly seen or cared for. When I met him, he showered me with attention and affection like no one ever had. He made me feel wanted and cherished, and for the first time, I thought, this must be what love feels like.

I wasn't physically attracted to him, but I told myself that love was deeper than that. It was about how someone treated you, how they made you feel safe. He seemed kind, generous, and emotionally available—everything I thought I needed. I believed attraction would grow. I believed he was good.

But early on, that illusion cracked.

One day, totally by accident, I stumbled upon his email account—it was just open on the screen. And this was the early days of the Internet. I'm talking dial-up, barely-anyone-has-Wi-Fi kind of early. Hacking wasn't even a real thing back then unless you were in a movie. And yet, right there in his inbox was a message to another girl, saying they had kissed. My heart dropped.

I confronted him, expecting at least some kind of honesty. But instead, he went full performance mode. He looked me in the eye and told me—completely seriously—that someone must have hacked into his email account and planted that message just to mess with him. As if some evil internet fairies were lurking around, waiting for me to accidentally open his email so I could see a fake confession of him cheating.

I wasn't even trying to catch him. I wasn't snooping. It was pure chance. So, for someone to hack him, just in case I happened to see it? It made no sense. But he stuck to that story with such confidence, such conviction, that I started doubting myself. Maybe I misunderstood. Maybe I was overreacting. That was the moment he rewrote reality—and it worked.

And it didn't stop there. For years, I brought it up again and again, needing clarity, needing to know I wasn't imagining it. Every single time, he denied it. Said it never happened. Made me feel insane for even asking.

Then, years later, we were on vacation. The kids were with my parents, and we were drinking, a little tipsy, a little relaxed. And I just asked him. No anger, no fight. Just, "Can you please tell me the truth? After all these years, I just need to know I wasn't crazy. We're together, everything's fine, I just need peace."

And in that moment, he finally admitted it. He kissed her. The email was real. It wasn't a hack. It wasn't a misunderstanding. I had been right all along.

But by the time he said it, the damage had already been done. Years of second-guessing myself. Years of carrying the weight of doubt that he put on my back. That moment wasn't just about a kiss—it was the blueprint for everything that came after.

Chapter 2: All Surface, No Soul

After I found the email and confronted him, the gaslighting was so intense, so expertly manipulative, that I ended up apologizing to him. Me. Apologizing for having the nerve to question something I saw with my own eyes. That was the moment the dynamic was set. I would doubt myself, and he would always, always be the victim.

We kept dating, and slowly, more red flags started to show—ones I didn't even know how to name back then. He used to compliment himself constantly. At first, I thought it was just humor or maybe a shield to protect his insecurities—he was very overweight and seemed self-conscious. But over time, I realized that he genuinely believed he was perfect. Not "I'm doing my best" kind of perfect. I mean flawless. Untouchable. The smartest, funniest, most magnetic man alive—if you asked him.

He knew a lot of people—or at least he acted like he did. He was always "in" with someone, always had some random acquaintance to name-drop, and always made himself sound like this popular, well-connected guy. But none of his relationships were real. He had no true friends, no one who knew him deeply. Everything was surface level, even with me.

I started noticing that I couldn't have a meaningful, intelligent conversation with him. Nothing deep. Every time I'd ask for advice or just want to talk about life in a real, vulnerable way, he'd either make a joke or give some shallow, dismissive response. There was no emotional depth. No curiosity. No connection. Just noise.

And sex? It was terrible. I'm not saying that to be cruel—I'm saying it because it's part of the truth. No matter how gently or patiently I tried to guide him, explain things, or show him what felt good, he couldn't perform. And he made it my fault. He said I made him nervous. My wanting sex put too much pressure on him. Suddenly, I was the problem for wanting intimacy in a relationship. He made me feel like I was obsessed with sex. Like, I was the one ruining it. When really, all I wanted was a healthy, basic physical connection with the person I loved.

I was always the one initiating it. And it wasn't like I was throwing myself at him constantly—I wasn't. But still, I was always the one trying, making the effort, looking for closeness. And after a while, it just felt pathetic. I didn't want to feel like I was begging to be wanted. I wanted to feel like a woman. I wanted to feel desired. I wanted to be courted. Pursued. Held. He never gave me that. He never made me feel like I was someone to be touched or treasured.

So, I stopped, not out of anger, but out of defeat. I didn't want to keep putting myself out there just to be blamed or rejected. I didn't want to feel like I was pressuring someone to love me. And I didn't want to keep hearing that his dysfunction was somehow caused by me.

Eventually, I just stopped wanting it altogether. Because what's the point of wanting something that makes you feel worse every time you try?

I barely had orgasms with him. My body didn't matter. Only his comfort did.

As I pointed out, I wasn't attracted to him. But I told myself that attraction would grow, that it didn't matter because he was such a "good person." I made peace with the idea that I would just live an unsatisfying sex life. That this was love, and I should be grateful.

But looking back, I don't even know what I was holding on to. He wasn't kind. He wasn't supportive. He wasn't generous or emotionally available. So, what was I seeing? Why did I still believe there were good sides to him?

Maybe it was because I wanted love so badly. Maybe it was because I didn't grow up knowing what real love looked like. When you come from a childhood where warmth and safety are missing, you learn to cling to anything that feels like stability, even when it's just an illusion.

He was my first relationship, and I wanted it to work. Not because I was naive or foolish, but because I believed in commitment. Because I believed that if I gave enough, loved enough, and sacrificed enough, it would turn into something beautiful. That it had to. I needed to believe that someone would finally choose me. Stay with me. Love me the way I have never been loved before.

And he knew that. He sensed it, and he used it.

He sold me a version of himself that was confident, charming, and powerful. He played God in his little world—and I was just trying to make sense of mine. When you're vulnerable, when you've been starved of love, you don't always see manipulation for what it is. You see hope. You see potential. You see something you want to be true.

And when you've been emotionally conditioned to believe that your needs are too much, your standards too high, you stop asking for more. You convince yourself this is enough. This is what love looks like.

I didn't stay because I was weak. I stayed because I was loyal. Because I was hopeful. Because I believed people could grow. Because I didn't yet know that love isn't supposed to hurt like that.

So, no—I wasn't dumb for staying. I was doing what every person who's ever wanted to be loved does: I held on.

But holding on almost cost me everything.

Chapter 3: Convenient Amnesia

It didn't take long before I realized I was the one doing everything.

Not just the emotional Labor, not just the thinking, not just the feeling. Everything. Every adult responsibility, every practical detail, every call, every email, every task. He couldn't even bring himself to dial a number. If I asked him to call customer service, set up an appointment, or speak to someone about something, he'd say, "You're better at these things. You're so good with people." Like it was a compliment. Like it was flattery.

But it wasn't. It was laziness. It was entitlement. It was him outsourcing adulthood to me while pretending I was just more "talented" at it.

And it didn't stop at errands. He couldn't even handle putting a simple reminder in his phone. Ever.

He'd forget things constantly—things he promised to do, things I'd asked him to take care of—and every time I reminded him, it was the same script: "You never told me that." Or "We never talked about this." He'd act confused, offended, and innocent.

He didn't want to remember. Because forgetting gave him power.

If it wasn't written down if it wasn't scheduled, then it didn't exist—and that meant he could deny it. He could change the story. Rewrite the timeline. Escape responsibility. And if I pressed him? I was the one making things up. I was imagining conversations. I was the problem.

And God forbid I suggested he use his phone like a normal person—to set a reminder or jot something down in a calendar. Suddenly, I was nagging. Controlling. Overbearing. But the truth was, it was easier for him not to remember. Because if he never remembered, then he never had to show up.

He was also cold. Ice cold.

I could be sick. I could be in bed with a fever, in pain, exhausted—and he wouldn't even blink. He wouldn't ask if I needed anything. Wouldn't touch me. Wouldn't even look at me. I could've been dying, and he would've stayed on his phone like nothing was happening.

No warmth. No comfort. No empathy.

And the worst part? I started getting used to it.

I stopped expecting anything. I stopped asking. I stopped needing it. Because every time I showed a need, it was met with either silence or annoyance. So, I buried my needs. I buried myself. I was tired. Numb. Functioning on autopilot.

I was carrying both of us, and he still made me feel like I wasn't doing enough.

Chapter 4: The Proposal That Meant Nothing

For some reason, I always convinced myself that everyone has flaws, and no one is perfect. I clung to the times we laughed, the bare minimum of good moments. I kept believing it meant something. That it would grow into more.

And I wanted more. I wanted the relationship to move forward.

I started talking to him about moving in together. He made me look for apartments. I searched, I planned, I dreamed. But every time something real, something concrete was about to close, he'd back out. Always with the dumbest excuses. And somehow, it always became my fault.

He told me that if we moved in together, he'd just feel like a guest in my house. It made no sense. I wasn't trying to move him into my apartment—I was ready to leave mine. I was totally open to starting over, to finding a new apartment where we could design something together. A neutral place. A fresh start. I said it a hundred times: "It'll be ours."

But still—no.

"There won't be space for my stuff."

"It won't feel like my place."

Excuse after excuse after excuse.

I kept trying to make it work. To reassure him. To meet him halfway. But I was always talking to a wall.

I was living alone. He was still living with his parents. And I wanted a life. A real one. I wanted to get married. To have a normal relationship. I was pushing for something stable, something real. Something two adults build together.

Then—completely out of nowhere—he proposed.

No conversation. No buildup. No planning. Just, "Will you marry me?" And I said yes. Because I thought, finally. Finally, something was moving forward. Finally, he's showing me that he's serious.

I thought it was fine to be engaged and keep looking for an apartment together. I didn't expect a wedding the next day. I just wanted momentum. Progress. A plan.

We were engaged for a few months. I tried to involve him in the wedding planning. I wanted his opinion. His presence. Something. But every question I asked—about the venue, the timing, the guest list—was met with blank stares. Shrugs. Indifference. He never gave real answers. Never participated. Never seemed like he was actually in it.

He also never gave a clear answer about when we were going to move in together. And I was never going to marry him without living with him first. I wanted to see what life together would be like.

Then, just like he proposed—without warning—he canceled the engagement.

He told me his mother had found out about the wedding and threatened to cut him off financially if he married me. And just like that, he folded. He said we could keep dating, but call off the engagement. No moving in. No planning. No next steps.

He handed over the steering wheel of our relationship to his mother without hesitation.

And that was it.

That was the first time I said enough.

I left him.

Chapter 5: The Biggest Mistake of My Life

After I left him, I started doing okay. I had space to breathe, space to think. But I could never truly get rid of him. He didn't respect boundaries—not even a little. I had broken up with him, but he was still there. Always there. Texting me like nothing had changed. Making jokes. Trying to keep conversations going like we were friends. Like he hadn't just dragged me through emotional hell.

And I wasn't engaging. I wasn't flirting. I wasn't answering the door he kept knocking on.

I had even started seeing someone new. And for the first time in my life, I felt something different. I mean fireworks. Physical attraction. Emotional ease. It was light. Simple. There was no tension, no walking on eggshells. Nothing was hard.

But as soon as he saw that my relationship with the new guy was getting serious, he pushed his game to another level. He started emotionally pressuring me—hard.

He had no respect for my new relationship. He didn't care that I had moved on. He didn't care that I was seeing someone else. It was like, in his mind, my relationship was just a joke. A temporary distraction. It was obvious to him—for some reason—that I belonged to him, and he was going to get me back.

He became jealous. Possessive. Then came the emotional performances—he started saying all the right things. The man who had never shown real vulnerability was suddenly crying, apologizing, telling me he finally understood what he had lost. He showed up uninvited. Sent flowers. Made gestures—little things I had begged him for during our entire relationship, now performed like acts in a carefully planned show.

It wasn't love. It was a strategy. He knew exactly what to say. Exactly what I wanted to hear. Exactly how to wear sadness on his face, so I'd question everything.

And slowly, it started working. He chipped away at my clarity, at the progress I had made. He made me feel guilty. Like I was cruel for moving on. Like I owed him something for all the years we were together.

And eventually... I caved.

I broke up with someone who had shown me kindness, simplicity, and possibility. Someone who might have led me to something better.

And I went back.

To him.

The biggest mistake of my life.

Chapter 6: Back Where I Shouldn't Be

His act didn't last long.

All the energy he had spent getting me back—the tears, the flowers, the emotional speeches, the promises to change—all of it vanished the second he got what he wanted. The second I left a good man who could have made me happy, he dropped the mask.

He went right back to who he always was.

The lying. The manipulation. The way he twisted everything until I was the one apologizing. All of it came rushing back like nothing had ever changed. It was as if his only real goal was to make sure I didn't get away. Once I was his again, once I had given up something good for him, he didn't need to try anymore.

And on top of everything else, he had this bizarre tendency to lie about the smallest things. Pointless things. Things normal people wouldn't even think to lie about. I'd catch him lying about something insignificant—something there was no reason to hide—and when I confronted him, it was somehow my fault. He had to lie because of the way I asked, or the way I made him feel, or because "he didn't want to deal with my reaction." It was never just, "I lied." It was always spun into a justification that blamed me.

And when it came to arguments—God, that was a whole new level of mental warfare. Every fight followed the same exhausting pattern. He would shift reality to make himself the victim. If I confronted him about something he did, he'd somehow turn it around and blame me. If I brought up something we talked about or agreed on—something he promised—he would just look at me and say, "We never said that." And even when it came to the simplest things—just living life, doing the most basic, normal stuff—he would always say no. I'm not talking about wild requests or expensive plans. I mean regular things. Going to the supermarket together. Grabbing dinner. Taking a weekend off. Planning a vacation like normal couples in their early twenties do. It was always no. There was never a reason. Never an explanation. Just a cold, flat no. If I wanted to plan something fun or spontaneous or even a simple date night, he'd shoot it down like it was ridiculous. And not because I was nagging or being pushy. Not because I expected him to pay. I was more than willing to pay, to plan, to make things happen. I just wanted to experience life with him. Like people do when they're in a relationship. And the sickest part? The only time he would ever change that "no" into a "yes" was when I broke down. When I cried. When I had nothing left in me. After he had crushed every little plan, every bit of energy I had to create something good, then he'd flip it and agree, like he was doing me a favor. By then, I didn't even want to go anymore. It wasn't about pressure. It wasn't about me not accepting a "no." It was about being slowly conditioned to stop asking. To stop expecting anything. And eventually, I did. How many times can someone say no to joy before you stop trying to feel it? That's the thing people don't always see. It's not about the one "no." It's about the pattern. The erosion. The way it chips away at your spirit until you stop dreaming at all. It didn't matter if I had proof—texts, voice notes, or literal black-and-white evidence. He would flat-out deny it. Pretend like it never happened. Even when I could trace the whole conversation back step by step, even when I laid it out logically, he would still lie. As if by denying reality, he could make it disappear. And when I backed him into a corner with facts, when he had no way out, no defense left—that's when the silent treatment would begin. He would shut down the conversation completely. Not in a calm, I-need-a-minute way. I mean full emotional lockout. "I'm not here to prove anything to you." "I'm done with this conversation." And that would be it. He'd vanish. Shut off. Pretend I didn't exist. Meanwhile, I'd be left spiraling, knowing I was right, holding the proof in my hand, and still somehow feeling insane. That kind of manipulation? It drives you to the edge.

It gave me rage attacks I couldn't control, because the gaslighting was just too much. How do you stay calm when someone lies to your face about something you both know happened? And then—this is the most twisted part—he would use those moments against me. The ones where I broke. The ones where I snapped after being emotionally stonewalled, lied to, and erased. He'd point to those as proof that I was unstable. I had anger issues. That he was the calm, rational one, and I was the unhinged, emotional wreck. He created the storm and then judged me for getting wet.

Chapter 7: The First Pregnancy

Shortly after we got back together, we took a vacation. I was sick at the time, taking antibiotics, and I was also on birth control. No one had ever mentioned to me that antibiotics can interfere with birth control, and I had no idea I needed to be extra careful. So, I got pregnant on that vacation.

I didn't find out right away. I found out much later, at a very advanced stage of the pregnancy. And when I told him, his reaction was immediate: he didn't want the baby. He told me to have an abortion.

But I didn't want that. I wasn't a teenager—I was in my twenties. I had a difficult childhood, and for the first time in my life, I wanted to feel like I could build a family. I was scared, yes—but also excited. I wanted this baby.

Because of how far along the pregnancy already was, I had to make decisions quickly. I needed his input. I needed a conversation. But instead of stepping up, he vanished.

He disappeared without a word. For two weeks. His phone was disconnected. No texts. No emails. No explanation. He was just gone.

During those two weeks, I reached out in every way I could. I texted, called, and emailed— pleading with him just to respond. Not to argue.

Not to fight. Just to talk. I needed to know what we were going to do. In every message, I laid out plans—how we could raise the baby together, how I was willing to take on the responsibility, how we could make it work.

I heard nothing.

About a week into his silence, his brother messaged me on MSN Messenger. His message was short and vague: "He's okay." That was it. No mention of the pregnancy. No concern. Just a status update. I hadn't told his brother about the pregnancy, but I begged him to ask his brother to contact me. I was running out of time. He said he'd try.

Another week passed. Then, finally, I got a message. He said he was coming back. We agreed to meet that evening.

When he came back, it wasn't like he was returning to something that mattered. He took his time, showered, and acted like nothing had happened. I—and the pregnancy—felt like an afterthought.

Before we saw each other again, I messaged him one more time. I told him I wanted to keep the baby. That we had been together for years, and we could still build something. I asked him to just consider it.

But when we met that evening, his response was sharp and final.

"Are you crazy?" he said. "I'm not going to raise this baby. I'm not ready for that."

There was no discussion. No empathy. Just pressure.

He insisted I have an abortion. I was also under intense pressure from my parents. Emotionally exhausted, physically overwhelmed, and with time running out, I made a decision I didn't want to make.

I had an abortion.

Not because I changed my mind. But because I felt like I had no choice. I was isolated, unsupported, and trapped.

He didn't come with me. My mother did. And because the pregnancy was already so far along, there were complications. Just days later, I started bleeding heavily and uncontrollably. I lost so much blood that I had to be rushed into emergency surgery. I was hospitalized.

He didn't show up then, either.

He only came after the surgery was over. There was no hug. No comfort. No emotional support. Nothing.

I felt like I was watching it all happen from somewhere outside my body. Like I was observing someone else's life, not living my own. I had just lost a baby I wanted. My body was in pain. My spirit was numb. And the one person who should have stood by me—who helped create this life—was nowhere when it mattered most.

I didn't know how to move forward.

Chapter 8: Choosing to stay

I want to be very clear about something.

I'm not writing this book to paint myself as a victim. I know there were choices I made that kept me in this relationship. I know I should've left long before I did. I take full responsibility for that.

And if I'm being completely honest, there was also a part of me that kept thinking maybe, just maybe, with enough persistence, I could still make him change. What if I just loved him hard enough, if I was patient enough, if I proved myself enough, eventually he'd see my worth? Eventually, he'd become the person I needed him to be.

I don't know why I wanted that from him. I don't know why I clung to that relationship as if it were the only one I'd ever be allowed to have. I don't know why I didn't think I was worthy enough to start over with someone new. Or why I didn't believe I could build a life on my own.

But for some reason, I just wanted to make it work. I needed to make it work. I had convinced myself that if I could just hold it all together—if I could be better, quieter, more understanding, more forgiving—it would eventually be okay.

Looking back, I know now that that was my biggest mistake.

That was the part I took responsibility for.

I'm not saying I was perfect. Far from it. I made choices. I ignored the signs. I stayed when I should've walked. I held on when everything inside me was begging to let go.

And yeah… it was dumb.

But it was also deeply human.

After I stayed with him, everything we had once talked about—the idea of moving in together, the engagement, building a life—just quietly disappeared.

No conversation. No closure. Nothing.

It was as if, in his eyes, my decision to stay after everything that happened meant I had agreed to a new kind of relationship. One where he dictated the terms. One where we didn't live together. Where we didn't move forward. Where we just "dated"—on his schedule, by his rules.

And I didn't push back. I didn't ask questions. I didn't demand clarity. I just… rolled with it.

It slowly became the norm. I convinced myself that maybe not every relationship has to follow the same path. Maybe not everyone needs to get married. Maybe love could look like this—separate homes, no shared future, no commitment. I didn't like it. But I told myself it was fine. That this was just what my love life was going to look like.

But what I didn't understand back then—what I didn't have the language for—was that I was in the middle of severe emotional abuse.

He was gaslighting me constantly. Twisting facts. Denying things, he said or did. Making me question what was real and what wasn't. Every time I brought up something hurtful he had done, somehow, I ended up apologizing. Somehow, I became the villain in every story.

He always made himself the victim, and I the aggressor.

I would say something like, "You left me completely alone when I needed you most," and instead of acknowledging anything, he would go silent. Shut down. Walk away. If I tried to talk about the abortion—the trauma, the grief, the fact that I never wanted to go through with it—he wouldn't respond at all. Just silence. Like it never happened. Like, I was the problem for still carrying it.

Every time I tried to hold up a mirror and make him see the truth, he escaped. Emotionally disappeared. And I'd be left spinning, questioning if I was wrong for even bringing it up.

This wasn't miscommunication. This was manipulation.

This was emotional abuse.

Chapter 9: The Erosion

He spent years conditioning me to believe that he was the best I could ever have.

The things he used to brainwash me sounded like this:

"You'll never find someone who accepts you like I do."

"No one else would be able to handle you."

"You're too emotional. You always overthink everything."

"You're lucky I'm still here after everything."

"This is just how I am—if you can't handle it, that's on you."

He also used my relationship with my parents against me. He'd say things like, "If even your parents don't want you, who will?" He'd tell me that I was lucky someone like him still "stood" me, and that if I ever dared to leave, he would make sure my biggest fear came true—that I'd end up completely alone. He even said my parents preferred him over me.

He didn't need to scream or insult me directly. He chipped away at me slowly, over time, with silence, with passive-aggressive remarks, with carefully timed disappearances, and with words that sounded almost reasonable but were designed to shrink me.

He made me feel like I was too much and not enough at the same time. Like I should be grateful for whatever scraps of attention he offered. Like, I was the unstable one. The difficult one. The one who should be thankful someone like him would "put up with me."

And so, I stayed.

Not because I was happy. Not because I was blind.

But because I was emotionally broken down to the point where I didn't trust my reality anymore.

And... because I was scared.

I was so scared of starting fresh. Of opening myself up to someone new. After everything I had been through with him—the highs, the crashes, the investment of years and energy—I was exhausted. I couldn't imagine starting over, building trust again, going through that terrifying unknown.

I had convinced myself that I needed someone to survive. That being in a relationship was better than being alone. I didn't know then that I could survive on my own. That I had myself, and that was enough. I didn't know how strong I was, because all he ever did was convince me I wasn't.

Looking back now, I see that I could have thrived alone. I didn't need him. I didn't need anyone.

But back then, I couldn't see it.

And the hardest part? I had no one to talk to about any of it. I had no safe place to say, "This doesn't feel right," and hear, "You're not crazy."

My relationship with my mom was practically non-existent. And I'm not here to blame her. I'm not here to bash her. But she's just not the kind of person you can have deep, emotional conversations with. She minimizes everything. Shrinks it down. Makes it sound like it's not a big deal. Maybe it's because narcissism is very difficult to understand, so it wasn't her fault.

Whenever I tried to talk to her, she would brush it off. Encourage me to "stick it out." Say things like, "Every relationship has its problems," or "He seems like a good man." And to her, he was a good man. He performed perfectly around her. Kind, thoughtful, polite. Salt of the earth.

She never saw what I lived with.

Yes, she was angry at him about the abortion. That was the one time I saw her react. But even then, it was like she bounced back quickly to, "He's not that bad."

And so, I stopped talking.

I stopped reaching out.

What's the point of sharing pain if no one around you sees it as valid?

I was isolated. Emotionally homeless. Seen by no one.

And when you have no one saying, "This isn't okay," you start to believe maybe it is. Maybe I am the problem.

But that's the thing—emotional abuse doesn't always show up in big, dramatic moments. He never exploded, never hit me, never screamed in public. What he did was smaller. Subtle. But relentless.

He pushed emotional buttons constantly. Little jabs, little criticisms, little lies, little manipulations. He chipped away at me in small, invisible ways—but he did it constantly. Consistently. Repetitively. He'd say something that stung and then play it off as a joke. He'd deny a promise he made and make me feel crazy for remembering it. He would withhold affection when I needed him most and act like I was the cold one.

He'd brainwash. He'd gaslight. And he did it on a loop.

And because the abuse came in tiny doses over time, when I did reach a breaking point and tried to vent to my mom, it always came out sounding like I was losing my mind over something "small." I'd say, "He did this, he said that," and she'd look at me like I was the problem. Because she didn't know about the hundred things that came before that moment.

She didn't see the pattern. She didn't understand the buildup.

And I didn't confide in her every time—it wasn't safe emotionally. But sometimes I would reach a limit. After being poked and prodded and gaslit for days, I would break. I would spiral into anger and confusion, and just need someone to hear me. To validate that it wasn't okay. So, I'd call her. I'd tell her about a fight. And she'd say, "That's what you're so upset about?"

Yes. That. And the hundred things before it.

But no one saw those hundred things. No one saw the slow erosion. They only saw me—angry, overwhelmed, emotional. And it made me think I was the problem. That I was unstable. That I was the toxic one. Because everyone around me seemed to be saying, "This is fine. You're not."

And when you're told that long enough, you start to believe it.

Chapter 10: A Child Without a Home

After a while, I started asking myself—is this it?

Am I going to be in this kind of relationship forever? No progress. No living together. No marriage. No future. Just… this?

So I told him that. I told him I wasn't okay with this version of love that never moved forward.

And that's when he surprised me.

It was a few years after the first pregnancy—the one he pushed me to end—and suddenly, he was the one suggesting we have a baby. Out of nowhere. He said it like it was the most natural thing in the world.

And I remember looking at him and saying, "Are you serious?"

A couple of years ago, he practically forced me to have an abortion. He disappeared when I needed him most. And now, he wanted to have a baby?

He told me he had no problem having a baby with me, as long as the relationship stayed exactly as it was.

No marriage. No living together. No shared home.

Just… him helping with the baby in his way.

He said we live in a "progressive" world. Not every relationship needs to follow the mold of a couple living together. That this could work.

And I know—I know how that sounds.

I'm not writing this to make myself a victim. I'm not saying I didn't have a choice. I'm saying I didn't have the tools to make a healthy choice. I didn't have the emotional logic to see what I was stepping into.

I came out of a broken home. A place where love was conditional, and safety was inconsistent. I grew up longing for something real, something warm, something that felt like a family. And when I left that environment, I clung to the first person who showed me any version of love, even if it was warped, inconsistent, and damaging.

I had always wanted to be a mother. That part of me was real. Deep. Sacred. And somewhere in my broken thinking, I convinced myself that maybe I could build something out of this. Maybe I couldn't have the love I wanted. Maybe I couldn't have the life I dreamed of. But at least I could have a child. At least something would come out of everything I had been through. At least this pain would lead to something.

So I agreed.

I agreed to have a baby in a relationship that didn't make sense, with a man who had never shown up for me, in a setup that went against everything I ever imagined for my life.

I agreed not to live together. To not get married.

Because in my trauma-wired brain, it still felt like a step forward.

I know that someone with a healthy upbringing—someone with a clear sense of self-worth—would have said, "Go f** yourself."

And walked away.

But I wasn't that person. Not then.

I didn't have that logic in my brain.

All I had was a deep ache for love, a dream of motherhood, and a desperate hope that maybe this would make everything I had endured… worth something.

And we got pregnant.

On the very first try.

At that point, I had kind of already given up on the idea of a "normal" relationship. I convinced myself that not every pot has its lid, and maybe I just wasn't meant for marriage or romantic love. Maybe that wasn't in the cards for me. Maybe I wasn't meant to be loved; I was meant to be a mother.

That thought gave me some kind of purpose. Some kind of hope. I told myself, "Maybe if I can't have love, I can still have a child. Maybe that's what will fill me."

Our relationship at that stage was incredibly shallow. There was no effort from him to get closer. No warmth. No excitement about the baby coming. And then, just when I thought I couldn't be more disrespected, he told me he would require a paternity test once the baby was born.

He didn't trust me. He didn't value me. He wanted a child, but he didn't even believe the child was his. But I let it slide because I was already so emotionally worn down that I barely reacted.

Then the time came—I gave birth. And I did it completely alone.

I was in the delivery room for three days. Three days of contractions and no dilation. Three days of pain, and no one could give me an epidural. Three days of agony. He wasn't there. He visited briefly here and there, but mostly he was "at work." Even when he was present, he wasn't with me. He sat on his phone while I was curled up in pain, not even offering a hand to hold. No hug. No comfort. Just indifference.

What kind of man doesn't take time off work when his child is being born?

When the baby went into distress, I had to be rushed into an emergency C-section. I called my mom. My mom called him. He came after the baby was born. After the surgery. After I had gone through it all alone.

And when was I discharged from the hospital? He dropped us off at home and left. I was in pain. I was terrified. I was trying to care for a newborn, barely able to move, crying constantly. I had what I now recognize as mild postpartum depression, but I had no space to process it. No time. No support.

Every diaper, every fever, every sleepless night—I handled it on my own. He said he'd be there. That we'd raise the baby "together." But the reality was, every time I called him to help, he had an excuse. He had to work. He was busy. He'd "try" next time. But the next time never came.

I was completely on my own. No help. No rest. No partner.

In hindsight, I now understand what his suggestion was about. He could sense that I was fed up—that I was pulling away. And losing control over me was his greatest fear. Controlling me had always been his bread and butter. So, he came up with a plan to tie me to him forever, without ever needing to commit to anything real.

He didn't want a baby because he wanted to be a father. He didn't care about continuing his name—he didn't even give our daughter his last name. She and our second son, who came later, both carry mine.

He used the one thing he knew would reach me: my longing for love and family. That was the real reason he brought up having a child. Not out of love. Not out of hope. Just control.

Chapter 11: The Trap

Then, when our baby turned six months old and it was time for me to go back to work, I told him: "We need to figure this out. I need to work. We need to share daycare pickups, doctor visits, and responsibilities." But he refused. He told me I was irresponsible for wanting to work when the baby was still "so small." He said no good mother puts a six-month-old in daycare.

So, I quit my job. I gave up a career I had just started to build. I had been rising at my workplace. I was doing well. And I walked away from all of it—because I had no choice. Because he wouldn't help. Because if I didn't do everything myself, nothing would happen.

And that was when the true control began.

Now that I had no income, I became financially dependent on him. He controlled everything—what to buy, when to buy, how to buy. He wouldn't even let me get a driver's license. He said it "wasn't necessary." He didn't let me take driving lessons. He decided what I could and couldn't do.

And little by little, I was erased.

I was a mother, yes—but I was also a woman cut off from the world. From independence. From freedom. From myself.

I know this is what I said I wanted. I know I agreed to have a baby with him under those conditions. But I didn't realize then how deep the trap would go. He knew exactly what he was doing. He knew how to build the perfect setup to control me, and I walked right into it.

And that's when the emotional abuse became even worse. As if everything before wasn't already enough.

The only income I had at that point was Social Security, and the entire amount went straight to rent. My rent. I wasn't living with him. I wasn't supported by him. I was barely surviving, and everything I had went to keeping a roof over our heads.

Every other expense? I had to ask permission. He controlled what I could and couldn't buy. I had no clothes. I barely had any underwear. And even that didn't feel like a priority, because I couldn't go anywhere anyway. I couldn't afford to. I didn't have a life outside the walls of my home.

Whenever I wanted to step outside—to breathe, to meet a friend, to just air out for an hour—I'd ask him to come and stay with the baby. And every time, his answer was the same: "I'm too tired from work." He never helped physically with the baby. Never gave me a break. And because of that, I had no time, space, or freedom to create a social life of my own. I was a mother, 24/7, behind closed doors. That was it.

Eventually, even wanting to go out felt pointless. I didn't need clothes—I had nowhere to wear them. I had one pair of jeans and two T-shirts I could wear outside and not feel completely ashamed. The rest were just old rags I wore around the house. Because I never left the house.

It wasn't just physical isolation—it was emotional starvation. It was the slow erasure of who I had been before motherhood, before this relationship. I started to forget what it was like to have an identity beyond "mom." I wasn't a woman with dreams, or plans, or a future. I was just someone surviving—barely.

And still, when I told him I wanted to go back to work, he blocked every path I tried to create. Daycare costs money—money I didn't have. I offered a solution: "Let's split the cost. I'll work. I'll contribute. I just need a little support to get started." He said no.

He wouldn't help pay for daycare. It wouldn't help pick up the baby. Wouldn't adjust his schedule. He said daycare past 1:00 p.m. was too expensive, and he wouldn't pay a cent more. So what did that leave me with? I was expected to find a job from 8:00 a.m. to 12:30 p.m.—just enough time to drop the baby off and get her out before the subsidized hours ended.

But those jobs don't exist. Not meaningful ones. Not ones that allow a person to build independence, to grow, to dream again. He knew that. That was the point. He blocked every exit and handed me just enough rope to make it look like I was choosing this life.

So, I stayed home.

Not because I wanted to—but because I had no other option.

And yet, through all of that—through all the exhaustion, the loneliness, the control—there was one thing that saved me: my daughter.

Being a mother gave me something to hold on to. From the very beginning, we had an unbreakable bond. She was the light in my world. She gave me purpose. Love. Real, pure love. That was the only thing that brought me joy.

Chapter 12: No Way Out

One night, when he was at my house, he suddenly became all lovey-dovey, and I let my guard down.

He initiated sex.

I told him no, not because I didn't want to be close, but because I wasn't on birth control. After giving birth, I struggled with hormonal imbalances and wasn't taking anything at the time.

I asked him to use protection.

He refused.

He told me condoms didn't work for him. That he couldn't perform with one. And instead of respecting my body, instead of choosing to connect in a safer, more respectful way, he made a promise: "Don't worry. I'll finish outside."

He didn't.

And just like that, I was pregnant again.

By this point, the financial abuse had gotten worse, much worse.

I wasn't allowed to have a bank account. I had no access to money of my own. And yet, somehow, I was constantly blamed for spending money. I never understood it—what money was I supposedly spending? I didn't buy anything. I didn't shop. I didn't even have proper underwear. But he'd throw accusations at me about being financially irresponsible, about "wasting" money.

He controlled every detail of our finances. Even the grocery shopping. He never let me go alone. He decided what to buy. What he thought was necessary. If I asked for anything that wasn't on his list—something I needed, something small, something for myself—it became a debate about how careless I was with money. As if a box of cereal or a bottle of shampoo were a luxury.

And I wasn't asking for extravagance. I wasn't begging for vacations. Sometimes I just wanted to take our daughter on a small trip. Not even an overnight—just a day trip, to get out of the house, to breathe. Especially while I was pregnant and exhausted and mentally drained. But every time, the answer was the same: "We don't have gas money. I'm not paying for gas."

He'd say, "If you want to go somewhere, you'll have to pay for the gas yourself."

But I had no money. Not a dime to my name.

By then, my friendships had already started to fade away. People stopped inviting me to things. They couldn't understand why I never came. But the truth was—I couldn't. He never helped with our daughter. And later, with our son, it was the same. I couldn't go out. I couldn't take time off. I couldn't do anything.

All the parenting. All the sleepless nights. All the doctor's appointments. Every diaper, every fever, every emergency—it was all on me.

At the same time, he had been living in an apartment that his parents gave him. It wasn't his—technically it belonged to his sister, who was living abroad—but it was where he lived for about a year. And during that entire time, I would ask him, "Why can't we just live there together?"

He always said the same thing: "This is just temporary. She'll be back. The apartment isn't mine."

And eventually, about a year later, he did move back in with his parents.

So, there I was—living alone in my apartment, pregnant, raising a toddler, without help, without money, without support.

And then I gave birth to our second baby.

It started fine. I had a scheduled C-section. Everything seemed okay.

But that night—around 11 p.m.—a sea of doctors flooded into my hospital room. I'll never forget the look on their faces. They told me my newborn son had a life-threatening heart defect. He needed surgery. He was being transferred to the ICU immediately.

I was terrified. Shaking. Hysterical.

I called him.

I expected him to say, "I'm coming. I'm on my way."

I expected him to jump in the car and come be with me. With our son.

But all he said was:

"Okay. Keep me posted."

And then he went back to sleep.

I was left alone in the NICU with a newborn hooked up to more tubes than I can describe. Machines beeping, monitors blinking, my son's tiny body lying there—and no one beside me.

A few days later, we were transferred to another hospital for his heart surgery. I had a toddler at home. I was still recovering from a complicated C-section. My son had to be intubated—he couldn't even breathe on his own. And I was juggling hospital shifts, motherhood, emotional collapse—everything—on my own.

He barely showed up. Maybe once.

No help. No support. No presence.

His excuse was always work.

Always work.

But what hurt even more was how he started crafting this narrative—to everyone else—that he was "doing it all." That he was the hero. That he was financially supporting his family on his own. He was the strong, dependable father figure who held everything together.

He made himself look like "father of the year" while I was drowning. Alone. With two children. Post-surgery. Sleepless. Scared. Fighting for our son's life while he posed for sympathy and praise.

By this point, the financial abuse had escalated to a whole new level.

I still technically had a bank account from the time before I lost my independence, and I had old loan payments I was responsible for. But I couldn't afford them. I had no income of my own. No way to keep up.

After our second child was born, my Social Security income increased slightly. And at that point, he agreed to cover the loan payments—but under his conditions. He made me transfer every single dime from my Social Security payments directly to him.

So, the only money I had—my income—went to rent and paying him back for "helping" with my loans. He told everyone he was paying them for me as if he was doing some huge favor. But the truth is—I paid him back. Every cent.

That became the pattern. He would use anything he "gave" me as leverage later, twisting the story to make himself the hero, the provider, the man who "did it all." I had nothing. No access. No freedom. No support.

I was emotionally and physically drained. I had a toddler. I had a newborn son. I had no help. And still, he was parading himself around like Father of the Year. Boyfriend of the Year. Supporter of a family. A martyr. While I sat at home, alone, surrounded by four walls, empty.

I was depressed. I couldn't even bring myself to clean the house. I was running on fumes. And I remember one moment so clearly sitting there, with both kids asleep, looking around the apartment, and thinking, "This isn't living."

That's when I told him: I want to leave you.

And just like that, he revealed the newest weapon he could use to keep me stuck: my children.

The only thing I ever truly loved—the only light in my life—was being a mother. And he knew that. He used it.

He told me if I left, I'd end up in the gutter. That no one would want me. That I'd be like "an ape living in trash."

He said he would take the kids away from me. That I had no money, no job, no stability.

He said no judge would ever give custody to someone like me. That I hadn't worked in years. That I had no future, no value.

And I believed him.

I didn't know about legal aid. I didn't know about resources. I didn't have the strength or knowledge to fight. I was terrified.

So, I stayed.

For years.

Every time I threatened to leave, he threatened to take the kids. And I couldn't risk that. I couldn't risk losing them. They were the only thing keeping me going.

Eventually, the isolation became complete. He had already pushed away my friends. But now, I was growing more and more distant from my own family, too. To them, he was the responsible one. The man who paid the bills. The involved father. The one who stepped up.

They couldn't understand why I would want to leave him.

And honestly? I stopped explaining. I didn't fully cut contact, but I stopped opening up. I stopped sharing. Because what's the point of telling people how bad things are when no one believes you?

And then one day, I was sitting on the floor, playing with my son, and a thought came to me out of nowhere:

"If I died today, no one would show up to my funeral because no one knows who I am."

That's how isolated I had become.

No friends. No emotional connection to my family. No partner. Just me. Trapped. Drowning in a version of life that felt more like slow death.

And that's when I knew: I was done.

Not in a rage. Not in a dramatic fight.

Just a quiet, heavy, final kind of done.

I told him I was breaking up with him.

And I left.

What I didn't know was that my real nightmare was only just beginning.

After I left him, I tried everything I could to keep things civil, for the sake of the kids.

I didn't want to go through court. I didn't want a messy legal battle. I was willing to go through a mediator. I told him I was fine with any amount of child support he was willing to offer. I wasn't trying to ruin his life. I wasn't trying to bleed him financially. I just wanted stability, clarity, and some kind of structure for our children.

I wanted him to take responsibility.

I wanted him to be in their lives—not just in theory, but for real. Present. Active. Accountable.

I told him I wanted an official agreement—something that said he would take the kids for at least one weekend a month. Just once a month. A simple sleepover. Something that would allow me even the tiniest bit of space to think, to rebuild, to breathe. I needed that time. Not for fun. Not for travel. Just for survival. For self-development. To find work. To plan a life.

He laughed in my face.

He said, "I would never take them for two nights a month. Are you insane?"

And then, he said the line I'll never forget:

"If you want anything from me, go sue me. Get a lawyer."

He knew I had no money for a lawyer. He knew I had no support. I didn't even know legal aid existed. He knew I had no access to resources, and he weaponized that knowledge against me.

So I stayed stuck. Again.

With two kids.

Alone.

And he was completely absent.

He refused to take any regular part in their lives. No routine. No involvement.

Yes, he paid the rent, but always under conditions. It was leverage, not support. And any time he got angry, he'd say:

"That's it. I'm not paying rent next month."

That's why I wanted a legal agreement. I didn't even want him to pay my rent anymore. I didn't care. I wanted structure: monthly child support and a basic visitation schedule.

But he wouldn't have it.

He knew exactly what he was doing. He knew he had the upper hand.

And he didn't care that the kids were suffering. He didn't care that sometimes we had no food. I'd send him pictures of our empty fridge. That our kids needed help. That we needed help.

He just didn't care.

And then COVID hit.

And I went through all of it alone.

Lockdowns. Isolation. No money. Two small children. No help.

But then… something shifted.

All of a sudden, he changed.

He became nice.

He became present.

He started showing up for the kids. He became softer. Kinder. More attentive.

He even began to be emotionally available to me.

I was in shock. It was like I was dealing with a different person.

He came over one day, sat me down, and said,

"COVID made me realize the error of my ways. I see how badly I treated you. I see how I abandoned the kids. I want to be there now. I want to make it right."

Suddenly, he was making coffee plans. Workout plans. Parenting plans. Relationship plans.

"Let's go out."

"Let me take you for a walk."

"Let's build a future."

"Let me show you the man I've become."

I hadn't been with him in years. I had truly thought that part of my life was over. I was surviving alone, scraping by, parenting without rest. And then suddenly... this.

It wasn't just a reunion. It was every fantasy I had ever clung to.

It was the version of him I had begged for. Prayed for. Waited years for it.

I started developing feelings for him—real feelings. I started seeing a version of love I thought I would never have. I even became attracted to him—something I had never truly experienced before. He was affectionate. He was helpful. He was supportive. He was everything I had been starving for.

We started sleeping together again.

There were hugs. Conversations. Intimacy.

We exercised together. Took walks together. Did things as a family.

He played the part of a present father and partner flawlessly.

And I truly thought—this is it.

This is what all the suffering was for.

This is the reward. The miracle. The family I dreamed of finally came to life.

But it wasn't.

It was manipulation.

It was another setup.

It was love bombing at its finest.

And I didn't know it yet.

But I was walking straight into the next chapter of my nightmare.

Chapter 13: The Final Fall

One day, I was sitting on the balcony with my daughter. We were talking, just the two of us. And I remember saying how proud I was of her father for changing. For being present. For treating us with kindness and finally giving us the love we had needed for so long.

And then, without any warning, she looked at me and said:

"Mommy... I saw Daddy texting someone in his car."

She told me he had this little screen on the dashboard where the messages popped up. He didn't even try to hide it from her. She saw everything.

He was calling another woman "honey."

My stomach dropped.

I confronted him. And it all came out.

The whole time he had been rebuilding our relationship—telling me he loved me, sleeping with me, parenting beside—he had been in a relationship with someone else.

He played the victim, of course. Said I wasn't emotionally available. That she was younger—ten years younger—and didn't have kids, so she could give him "what I couldn't." In her eyes, he was a king. That she gave him full attention and made him feel like a man.

And I just sat there, thinking:

We just got back together. We have two kids. I'm carrying the weight of everything, and now you're comparing me to a childless 20-something?

Then he had the nerve to make it about him. Said he "couldn't decide between us." That he was "torn." He needed time to choose.

I said no.

No. No more choices. No more games.

Either you leave her and stay, or you walk out and never touch me again.

The next day, he came back. Soft. Sweet. Loving.

He touched me again. Told me he was choosing us.

I believed him.

I wanted to believe him.

I was so broken, so afraid of being abandoned again, so terrified of being that stupid, that gullible, that alone—that I apologized to him.

For everything.

For things I didn't even do.

For things he made up.

For having "anger issues," for "not loving him enough," for "not being available."

When I was the one who had been emotionally and financially abused for years.

But I couldn't bear another heartbreak.

So I let him in.

I let myself believe he left her.

I told him clearly:

"I will never have sex with you if you're with another woman."

He promised he wasn't.

We slept together again.

I told him it was all I had ever wanted—to feel loved by him, supported, held.

And then… that same evening… he told me the truth.

Not only had he not broken up with her, but he had chosen her.

He told me the last time we were intimate was "just friendly."

He said he wanted to keep seeing me, but as a friend.

He said she gave him things I never could.

That she "sexually woke him up."

She helped him realize what a bad father he had been.

And that she changed his life.

He said all of this after using my body, after using my heart, after pulling me back in only to spit me back out.

And I broke.

I shattered.

I felt so stupid. So, used. So utterly humiliated and discarded that something inside me just... shut down.

That night, I tried to take my own life.

I swallowed a full bottle of sleeping pills.

He had the kids that day. He came back to the apartment and found me unresponsive.

And instead of calling for help, he told the kids:

"Try to wake Mommy up. I must go."

And he left.

My children tried for two hours to wake me.

Eventually, they called my parents.

And that was when people finally understood the depth of what I had been going through.

When I was already on the edge of death.

It wasn't just a breakup.

It wasn't just cheating.

It was the final act in a long play of psychological abuse designed to wreck my self-worth.

To make me feel like I had nothing.

Like I was nothing.

And somehow... I survived.

Chapter 14: The Edge and the Climb

By then, I was so deeply traumatized by everything I had been through that I didn't even recognize myself anymore.

I wasn't suicidal again, but I was broken. I was suffering from severe depression and debilitating anxiety. The anxiety attacks were so intense that every time they came, it felt like I was dying. Like I was having a heart attack. I couldn't breathe. I couldn't function. I couldn't escape it.

And the only way I knew how to snap out of it… was to hurt myself.

I started cutting.

Every time the panic took over, I would lock myself in the bathroom, take out a razor, and cut myself. Not because I wanted to die, but because I needed something sharp enough to break the spiral. I couldn't let the kids see me like that. I needed to stop the attack, somehow.

And this happened frequently.

And he knew.

He knew I was hurting myself. He knew I was spiraling. And still, he fed off it. He fed off the power.

By then, I had developed real feelings for him. The kind of feelings I had been desperate to feel for years. I thought I was truly in love with him, for the first time in my life. And he knew that, too.

I was begging him to leave her. I was apologizing over and over for things I didn't even understand. Just to win him back. Just to stop the bleeding.

And then, as if this wasn't cruel enough, he said:

"Why don't I give you her number? You two can talk. She's sweet. Maybe you'll even be friends."

I was stunned. I was in disbelief.

He was suggesting that I become friends with the woman he was cheating on me with.

After everything.

After the self-mutilation.

After the suicide attempt.

After the collapse of my mental health.

And I said fine. I took her number. But not because I wanted to be friends.

Because I wanted to beg her.

I wanted to explain what he was doing.

I wanted to plead with her:

"Please let me have my family back. Please don't do this to me."

And when I reached out to her, do you know what she said?

"If you keep pushing him, you're going to push him away."

Just like that.

This girl, who knew nothing about me, who had no idea what I had been through, talked to me like I was the problem. Like, I was the one destroying something. Like I was desperate and unstable.

She had no idea she was speaking to someone who was barely holding it together.

Who was cutting to survive?

Who had tried to die?

And then he kept doing the unthinkable—he stayed in contact with me and kept telling me how wonderful she was. He praised her to me. Over and over. As if I weren't already shattered. As if I hadn't just survived the worst emotional violation of my life.

Eventually, I hit bottom.

And I knew—I needed help.

I saw a psychiatrist. I was diagnosed with PTSD, major depressive disorder, anxiety disorder, and self-harming tendencies. I started taking medication. And little by little, I started to feel again. To stabilize. To come back to myself.

That's when I realized:

This man cannot be in control of my life anymore.

Not emotionally.

Not financially.

Not legally.

I didn't have money for a lawyer. But I started researching. I found out about legal aid. I applied—and I got a free lawyer.

And I sued him.

I sued him for child support.

I sued for custody arrangements.

Because even after everything, I still believed the kids needed a father. Not him, as a partner. Not him, as a man. But their father, in some legal, structured way. So I could step away. So I could finally breathe.

And I won.

I got a child support agreement.

I got a visitation schedule.

For the first time, he was required to take the kids for sleepovers—because the court made him.

The lawyer wasn't the best—free legal aid rarely is. He wasn't aggressive, and he didn't cover everything. He didn't push for every protection I probably needed. But it was something.

It was a start.

And for the first time in years, the narrative started shifting back into my hands.

Chapter 15: When Power Slips

He had spent years avoiding any kind of legal agreement.

Because he knew—once there was a court order, his power would be gone.

No more threats.

No more conditional payments.

No more emotional blackmail.

No more control.

As soon as the legal structure took effect and his control started to slip, his rage exploded.

He couldn't accept the fact that he no longer had free rein over my life. So instead of stepping into his role as a co-parent and moving forward with his new relationship, he did the opposite: he began retaliating.

That's when the threats started.

I began receiving anonymous messages through a private app. The language was unmistakable—hostile, vile, and eerily specific. He demanded money—$10,000—claiming I "owed" him for what I had "done." The tone wasn't just aggressive. It was calculated. Sadistic.

He threatened that I would be watched. That people would be stationed outside my home. That I wouldn't know when or where—but that they would be there.

And it went even further.

The messages made explicit, graphic threats—implying violence, harassment, and even sexual assault. It wasn't just intimidation. It was psychological warfare.

And buried in those threats was a label meant to dehumanize me completely.

He called me a "golden bitch."

Not a gold-digger. Not even just a bitch.

But a term designed to paint me as someone who exists to exploit men, then destroy them, and now must be "punished" for it.

It was a threat soaked in misogyny and vengeance.

I knew immediately who had written it.

The tone. The cadence. The phrasing. It was him.

And I was right.

The police later confirmed the messages came from someone connected to him. It was enough to obtain a restraining order.

But he didn't stop.

He just changed his strategy.

He found out—through me—that he could apply for legal aid.

He lied about his financial status.

Hid his real bank accounts.

And just like that, he got a lawyer. For free. Just like I did.

But where I used the law to protect our children and create structure, he used it to attack.

He took old messages I had sent him during some of the worst moments of my life—when he had gaslighted me for days, broken me down, and pushed me to emotional collapse—and presented them as harassment.

He didn't include the context.

He didn't show the abuse that led to those outbursts.

He Photoshopped them to make it look like I sent them all in one day.

And the judge believed him.

I wasn't even there.

She granted him a restraining order without a hearing.

In her ruling, she wrote that I had 30 days to respond, once I was officially served by a court messenger.

But I was never served.

I only found out about the restraining order ten days before it expired.

I had no idea what to do.

I wrote to the judge. Explained I wanted to respond. I wanted to defend myself.

She wrote back that if I wanted to contest it, I'd need a lawyer.

I had three days to find one, sign an affidavit, and prove everything I said was true.

She said she didn't recommend I pursue it, because only ten days remained.

I was overwhelmed. Panicked.

And I didn't have the money for even a single legal document.

So I let it go.

I thought, "What difference could it make now? It's almost over anyway."

What I didn't know… was that this temporary restraining order—based on Photoshopped lies and no due process—would be waved around for years.

Used against me.

Spun into a story where I was the abuser.

Where was I dangerous?

Where I was unstable.

And that was his plan all along.

And when the court finally forced his hand—when he had to pay child support, when he was legally required to take the kids—he lost it.

Instead of accepting the reality, instead of stepping into his role as a father and moving on with his new girlfriend, he turned on me. Hard.

He told me he would do everything in his power to flip the story.

That I would be the one paying child support.

That he would take the kids.

That I would be the one to lose everything.

And he meant it.

Chapter 16: When Control Fails, Chaos Begins

The moment he was ordered to pay child support—the moment it touched his wallet—he became a different kind of monster.

He couldn't accept that he was no longer in control. That I had stood up for myself. The court had forced him to take responsibility. And instead of simply fulfilling his obligations and moving on with his new girlfriend, he chose to retaliate.

That's when the threats started.

I began receiving messages on Telegram—a platform that makes it easy to hide identities. The messages were anonymous, but I recognized the tone instantly. They weren't just hostile. They were cold, calculated, and terrifying.

He demanded I transfer him $10,000, saying I would "pay" for what I'd done.

And what was it that I had "done"?

I had dared to ask for child support.

He couldn't stand the idea of being held accountable. Of being forced to contribute financially. The second legal order required him to give even a fraction of what I had given emotionally, physically, and financially for years, and he snapped.

The messages threatened that people would be waiting outside my home every day. Not just to scare me. Not just to harass me.

But to sexually assault me.

He called me a "gold-digging bitch."

As if asking for help feeding our children was greedy.

As if surviving years of abuse made me a villain.

As if everything he had done was erased the moment he had to give something back.

I went straight to the police.

And the police were able to trace the threats back to him.

It was enough to obtain a 90-day restraining order.

And you know what?

Those 90 days were the quietest time of my life.

For the first time in years, I could breathe.

No threats. No manipulation. No power games.

Just silence.

It proved what I had always known:

When his control is removed, his chaos stops.

Chapter 17: The Breaking Point

Then came the day that pushed me over the edge.

It was legally his time to take the kids. I had been holding on all week, barely functioning, running a fever, and completely depleted. I hadn't slept in days. I was sick, overwhelmed, and desperate for even a few hours of rest.

But when the time came, he bailed.

He said he couldn't take the kids because he was on vacation with his girlfriend.

The same girlfriend he had cheated on me with. The same woman he manipulated into thinking I was insane.

And in that moment—sick, exhausted, pushed past my limit—I snapped.

There was a loophole in our parenting agreement that he exploited to get out of taking responsibility. And I lost it.

I went to her Facebook page and called her what I felt at that moment: a homewrecker.

Yes, it was impulsive. Yes, it was public.

But I was done.

I had been holding everything alone. I had done everything right. I had the agreement. I had gone through court. I had asked, begged, pleaded for structure—for support—for some kind of humanity.

And he was on vacation.

Or so he said.

The truth? He wasn't on vacation at all. He was home. Sleeping at his parents' house.

His mother later admitted it to mine. He made it all up.

And of course, he used that moment—my one mistake—to his advantage.

He sent her to court to file a restraining order against me.

She barely knew me. But the language in her complaint?

I recognized it.

It wasn't her voice. It was his.

He stood behind her, quite literally, as she claimed I was violent. He came to court with her, arm-in-arm, like a protective boyfriend, after never once supporting me through anything.

It was a theater. And he was loving every second of it.

But I had a lawyer. She didn't.

I explained everything to the judge—calmly, truthfully, and without shame.

How I had reached my breaking point.

How I had begged for his help.

How I had been pushed too far.

How I had lashed out—not from cruelty, but from pain.

The judge dismissed the restraining order.

And she even threw him out of the courtroom.

She said it was between me and her.

She saw something.

But the damage was done.

That woman never once gave me the benefit of the doubt. Not in court. Not over the phone. Not when I begged her to believe me.

I had told her—I was still sleeping with him.

That he had been trying to get me back.

That he had love-bombed me.

That everything between us had felt real and was real.

I had proof. Messages. Screenshots. Dates.

But she refused to see it.

Instead, she clung to his story—that I was a jealous, unstable woman. That I had imagined the relationship. That I was just some ex trying to ruin her happiness. That I was "cutting myself" and begging because I was obsessed.

She used the very confessions I had shared with her in vulnerability—my mental health struggles, my trauma, my self-harm—as ammunition against me in court.

And maybe worst of all, she believed him.

Not just in court, but in her heart.

She believed he had never cheated.

That we weren't together.

That I was the liar.

Even when I had the evidence, the timeline, the truth—she chose the narrative he gave her.

And that's what abusers do.

They isolate.

They manipulate.

They recruit others to see you as the problem.

They bait you until you break—and then hold up your brokenness as proof that they're the victim.

Chapter 18: $300,000 and a Shrug

By that point, I had already been dragged through one restraining order that he obtained against me based on distorted and manipulated messages, and another one that his girlfriend attempted and failed to get.

Then came the next move: a dramatic lawsuit to reduce his child support.

The documents read like a smear campaign. I was portrayed as a gold-digger who had supposedly never worked a day in her life. He claimed I had drained his finances on shopping, vacations, and luxury—painting a fantasy of some glamorous lifestyle that had never existed.

Meanwhile, he positioned himself as the struggling, humble father, barely getting by with only $10 in his account.

But then his lawyer slipped.

Included in the court documents—by mistake—were bank statements from accounts he had tried to hide.

And there it was: nearly $300,000 sitting untouched.

This was the same man who had refused to pay for food, ignored photos of our empty fridge, and insisted he couldn't afford basic child support.

The same man who had told me he moved out of his sister's apartment because she needed to sell it, when in reality, he had rented it out, collected the money, and sold it later for profit.

I had no idea. While I was choosing between formula and rent, he was sitting on six figures.

When we presented this evidence to the court, he panicked.

He moved to cancel the lawsuit.

But not with honesty. Not with accountability.

Instead, he claimed he was dropping the lawsuit because he didn't want to "escalate our feud."

A feud that only existed in his head. I wasn't feuding. I was surviving. I wasn't fighting him—I was defending myself.

Then he twisted the narrative even further.

He claimed that since I had once had a restraining order issued against me—even though it was long expired—it made him fear that if he moved forward with the lawsuit, I might "do something" to him.

That restraining order, the one he had pursued with fabricated evidence, was now his excuse for walking away, not because he was caught lying about his finances, but because he was suddenly scared.

It was another performance. Another manipulation.

He wasn't scared. He was exposed.

And instead of facing the consequences, he wrapped himself in victimhood once again.

Even with all of that—the lies, the forged financial story, the documents he submitted himself—the judge allowed him to cancel the case.

And for the thousands I had spent on legal defense, I was awarded just $400.

That was the cost of exposing the truth: four hundred dollars and a shrug.

I thought maybe that would be the end of it.

But then he filed another lawsuit.

And because every case in family court goes to the same judge, it landed right back on her desk.

Chapter 19: Court-Approved Character Assassination

After failing to reduce child support the first time, he came back with something much darker—something that shattered me completely.

He hired a new lawyer. The last one had accidentally exposed his hidden finances, so this time, he found someone with the same lack of integrity he has—maybe worse. Someone who, from the looks of it, would write whatever story you wanted, if the price was right.

This time, he wasn't just trying to reduce child support—

He was trying to cancel it completely by trying to prove that I was unfit to be a mother.

He didn't prove anything.

Because there was nothing to prove.

But that wasn't the point.

This wasn't just about money anymore.

This was about control.

It was about setting the tone.

It was about sending a message:

That no matter what happened, no matter how long we'd been apart, he would never let me live my life in peace.

That I would always be under threat.

That I should always be afraid.

It was his way of saying:

"I will control you until the day you die."

And the court gave him the stage to try.

He filed a lawsuit for Parental Incompetence.

This is from a man who had never raised his children.

Who had spent years dodging visitation, refusing to take them even on his legally obligated days?

Who was never there for hospitalizations, never present for milestones, and never involved in their lives—unless it was to threaten, lie, or control.

And then, as if that wasn't vile enough, he weaponized my medical history.

He used my PTSD diagnosis against me. Claimed I had cognitive deficiencies. Said I was mentally unstable and incapable of caring for my children.

He alleged I was violent. That I beat my children. That I was a prostitute.

That I was engaging in prostitution in front of them.

That I never brushed their teeth. That they lived in filth.

That they were neglected, unloved, and unsafe.

All of it was lies. Fabricated from zero.

There wasn't a shred of truth to any of it.

But he didn't stop at lying—he manipulated evidence. He forged messages.

For example, there was a day when it was his time to be with the kids. My daughter got sick at school, and her teacher tried to call him—he didn't answer. I had taken a sleeping pill that day, assuming I had no parental duties. I texted him, clearly and directly:

"I took a sleeping pill and I feel too high to get up and go get her—where are you?"

No response.

So I forced myself up, picked her up from school, and brought her to his parents' house so she would be safe when he got home. Then I went back to sleep.

He took that message, cut out all context, and presented only the part where I said I felt too high to move, painting me as a drug addict.

He said I used illegal drugs in front of my children.

He used the expired restraining order as "evidence" that I was violent.

He even submitted an old photo of a mosquito bite on his arm and claimed it was a scar from domestic abuse.

Meanwhile, I was the one who bore real scars.

From cutting. From survival. From years of abuse.

He also claimed I harassed his girlfriend.

He recycled the same lies, dressed them in more drama, and presented them with no evidence—because there was no evidence to present.

He didn't do this because he cared about the kids.

He did it because he couldn't stand paying child support.

Because he couldn't stand not having control over me.

Because he knew that threatening to take away the one thing I lived for—my children—would be the final blow.

And the worst part? The part that still makes my blood boil?

In that same lawsuit, he dared to claim that the children would be better off living with him and his girlfriend.

This woman, who had never raised a child.

Who had never been pregnant?

Who had never spent a single night worrying over a fever, a school problem, or a hospital stay.

Who had no bond with my children?

No maternal experience.

No history with them beyond the drama he had pulled her into.

And yet—he tried to present her as the better option.

As if motherhood is transferable.

As if you can just take children from their mother and drop them into the arms of a stranger because it suits your legal strategy.

And the worst part?

She rolled with it.

She accepted the role.

She let herself be used.

She stood by his side while he tried to erase me—as if my entire existence as a mother could be swapped out like furniture.

What destroyed me most was how long the court allowed this circus to continue.

I had to give up my medical privacy.

I had to endure home visits.

A social worker came to my house. To his house.

My children were interviewed. Observed.

Two years of living under a microscope.

Of wake up every day thinking, This could be the day they take my kids.

He accused me of being everything I'm not.

And the court let him.

When the social worker finally completed her evaluation, she wrote the truth:

That my children were healthy.

That my home was safe.

That I was a competent, loving, emotionally available mother.

That I was doing everything right.

She recommended no changes to the custody agreement.

One overnight a week. Every other weekend.

Exactly what it had been.

The judge accepted her recommendation.

Case closed.

But she never addressed the lies.

She never acknowledged the forged evidence.

She never punished him for dragging our family through hell.

We filed for legal fees after thousands of dollars were spent on defense.

After proving, line by line, that every claim was false.

That he had tried to ruin the life of the one parent these kids could count on.

And again, she refused.

No explanation.

No consequences.

And I was left with the bill. Again.

The only thing that mattered at that point was that my children were still with me.

That they hadn't been taken.

That the damage—at least on paper—wasn't permanent.

But the emotional damage?

The trauma of being painted as an unfit mother?

The fear, the humiliation, the two years of living like my children could be taken away at any moment?

That stays with you forever.

And for what?

Because I asked him to be in their lives?

Because I dared to ask for support?

If I had known this was what we would go through, I never would've asked for child support.

I never would've asked him to show up.

I would've done it all alone from the beginning, like I had been doing all along.

But then again… if I hadn't fought for something legal, he would've always had the power to show up whenever he wanted, cause chaos, and disappear again.

So I did what I had to do.

And I survived.

Chapter 20: The Line I Wouldn't Cross Again

I could have let it destroy me again.

After everything—after the lawsuits, the defamation, the endless courtroom games, the attempts to rip my children away—I could have let it drag me back down. There were moments I wanted to. Moments, I felt the panic building, the old urge rising—the one that once made me reach for a razor just to quiet the storm in my head.

But this time, I didn't.

This time, I drew a line.

No more self-harm.

Not because the anxiety went away—it didn't.

Not because I wasn't broken at times—I was.

But because I refused to let this man carve any more pain into my body.

He had already taken so much.

He was not going to take that, too.

And even though there were days I couldn't get out of bed… I did.

Even though there were mornings I felt paralyzed with fear… I moved.

I forced myself forward.

I got a job. Not just a job—a damn good one. I got accepted into a bank. Me. After all those years of being told I was worthless, unemployable, and cognitively impaired, I started building a life. And then I got promoted.

And promoted again.

Every time I rose, it was like something inside him cracked louder.

The more I thrived, the more desperate he became to pull me down again.

But this time, I didn't fall.

Yes, I was angry. Furious. At him. At the system. At every piece of paper that let him get away with it.

But I chose not to live in that place.

I refused to let my life become a monument to his revenge.

I was going to be free—even if I had to drag myself across broken glass to get there.

And I did.

I kept working.

Kept showing up for my kids.

Kept living.

That was my victory.

Chapter 21: When He Took Aim at Her Too

But just when it felt like he had run out of ways to come after me, he shifted his focus.

He turned to our daughter.

By then, she was a teenager.

Smart. Strong. Emotionally aware.

And we had a bond that nothing could shake—until he started trying to chip away at it.

I didn't notice it right away.

That's how parental alienation works—it's subtle and insidious.

But over time, it became clear. He was trying to do to her what he had once done to me.

Only she didn't play along.

She resisted. She stood up for me. She saw him for who he was.

And that made him furious.

So furious that one day, when she stood her ground, he raised his fist at her.

He didn't hit her, but he got close enough.

Close enough that she ran out of his house in fear.

Close enough that she stopped speaking to him for six months.

She was overwhelmed. Shaken. She started experiencing anxiety.

Because the one person she still wanted to believe in—her father—had become a source of fear and manipulation.

And just like he did to me years ago, he tried to win her back with crocodile tears and empty gifts.

But this wasn't about love. It wasn't about connection.

It was about control.

He couldn't control me anymore—so he tried to control her.

And here's where I made one of the hardest parenting decisions I've ever had to make:

I didn't stand in her way.

Even though I had every reason to.

Even though I had every legal right to report what happened.

Even though I knew going back to him would likely hurt her again.

I didn't forbid it.

Because I knew if I did—if I banned her from seeing him—one day she might look back and think, My mom kept me from my dad.

So I let her decide.

I gave her space.

I gave her support.

I told her I would stand behind her, no matter what.

And I meant it.

I told her, "If you want to forgive him, I'll support you. If you want to give him another chance, I'll be here. But if anything changes—if it ever feels wrong—I'll still be here. Always."

That was the safest choice I could make.

Not for him.

Not for me.

But for her.

And when she decided to open the door again—little by little—I didn't stop her.

I stayed her anchor.

Because that's what good parents do.

They don't force healing. They hold space for it.

Even when it hurts.

Chapter 22: The Price of Doing the Right Thing

So she decided she wanted to give him another chance.

And again—stupid me—for trying to do the right thing.

Because whenever she gave him another chance, he started manipulating her against me in the worst way possible.

And the saddest thing is that he succeeded.

He brainwashed her so well.

I saw my daughter changing in front of my eyes.

Turning into a robot.

Speaking his words.

Blaming me for things I've never done.

Not respecting my boundaries.

Talking like she had this emptiness in her eyes.

The girl I knew was gone.

And that nearly destroyed me.

We started having fights daily.

She got so rude to me.

It was like I had a mini version of him in my house.

That's what I got as a thank you for encouraging his daughter to have a relationship with him.

He completely alienated her from me to the point where I just couldn't take it anymore.

And one day, I snapped.

I wrote her a text message full of curses that I'm so ashamed of.

But she was so disrespectful—my girl, my best friend, my daughter—was talking to me like I was her enemy.

And I just snapped.

After everything we'd been through together.

After giving my life to my kids.

She was disrespecting me like I was nothing.

I cursed her like nobody's business.

It was the first time in my life that I snapped as a mother.

She went to him and showed it to him.

And of course, he didn't give me the same grace I gave him when he raised his fist at her.

He started working so fast.

He convinced her to go to the police and file a report against me.

That I was violent.

He pressured her so hard that she eventually agreed.

Later on, I found messages on her phone.

She didn't want to do it.

She didn't want to lie.

She said he was asking her to lie that I was violent, when I wasn't.

He convinced her that it was okay.

That she needed to lie.

That it wasn't a police report.

It would just help her get support.

That exaggerating would get her someone to talk to.

And she fell for it.

She went and filed a complaint against me with the police.

Chapter 23: The Day I Became the Monster in Her Eyes

I found out she filed that police report.

I got so nervous.

I texted her when she was at school and asked:

"Did you file a police report against me?"

She probably got nervous.

She started ghosting me.

I was begging her to answer. I just wanted to know what she said.

She wrote a message to him that I found out later.

She told him I found out about the report.

She was scared.

And what did he do?

He fed her more lies.

He told her not to answer me.

He told her I was coming to the school to beat her up.

And she believed him.

So scared, she talked to her teacher.

The teacher, not knowing the full story, called Child Protective Services.

And just like that, I wasn't allowed to see my daughter.

Because she was scared of me.

Because of him.

He got her so scared that she believed her mother was coming to hurt her.

A girl who had never feared me.

Who once saw me as her safe place.

Now I was the danger.

The system didn't ask questions.

Didn't wonder how a girl raised in love could suddenly believe she needed protection.

They just reacted to the fear.

And he was there.

When I arrived at the school, he was already there.

You should have seen the grin on his face.

He succeeded.

He took my child away from me.

Like he promised he would.

Chapter 24: The Relapse

I was done at that point.

This was the first time in years that I hurt myself again.

All of the therapy.

All the strength I had built.

All the years I spent crawling out of the hole he dug for me—

Gone.

The pain-the betrayal, the helplessness, the isolation—was louder than anything I could reason with.

He had finally crossed a line I didn't think could be crossed.

He didn't just want to control me.

He wanted to destroy the love between a mother and her child.

And for a moment...

He did.

But even in that darkness—

I survived.

Chapter 25: The Goodbye I Never Wanted to Say

I was done.

With him. With her. With all of it.

After everything I had poured into raising her—with love, sacrifice, protection—she now looked at me like I was the enemy. She let him twist her mind so deeply that she couldn't even see me anymore.

So I did what I never thought I would do.

I told her to go.

I told her:

"If I'm such a monster, if everything I've done means nothing to you, then go live with your father."

And she did.

Watching her leave—walking out the door of the home I built, the life I fought for—was like someone had amputated a part of me. I felt phantom pain in my own house. Her absence had a weight, a presence. It was unbearable.

But he? He used it.

That was the moment my daughter needed her father the most. A moment that demanded protection, comfort, and presence.

And he turned it into a PR stunt.

He called my mother—my mother—and told her that our daughter needed "the support of her entire family right now." That she was going through something so heavy, she shouldn't be alone.

He made it sound noble. Caring.

But it was all a cover.

Because that same night?

He had an event.

With his girlfriend.

So he dropped our daughter off at my parents' house like she was a package. Like she was a child without a mother, without a home.

He played the concerned father in front of my mother, then walked out the door and went to his social event like nothing had happened.

He used her pain as an excuse to do what he wanted.

And that's who he is.

Chapter 26: The Ones Who Should Have Helped

When I arrived at my meeting with Child Protective Services, I was still hoping—naively, perhaps—that someone would finally listen.

But the social worker assigned to me?

She wasn't there to hear me.

She was there to shut me down.

From the moment I walked in, she had already made up her mind.

I was talking too much. I was "emotional." I had "too much to say."

Never mind that I had been dragged through years of legal warfare and psychological abuse, and now my child was being turned against me—none of that mattered to her.

Every time I tried to explain.

Every time I tried to bring up the evidence.

Every time I tried to show what was happening, she would interrupt me.

She rolled her eyes.

She dismissed my words.

She made me feel like the crazy one.

So eventually, I gave up on her.

I looked her straight in the face and said:

"Do whatever the fuck you want. You're not interested in the truth. You're just here to check your boxes and move on."

But thankfully, not all was lost.

My daughter has been assigned a social worker.

Someone separate.

Someone who—at the very least—would give her a space to talk.

And I? I didn't stop there.

Because I still had one thing left that I could hold onto—my job.

And through my job, I had access to subsidized therapy services.

So I used them.

I got a therapist.

I got a parental coach.

It wasn't cheap—even with the subsidy, it was a stretch.

But I did it.

Because I wasn't going to lose my daughter without a fight.

Chapter 27: The Moment She Saw Him

So that psychologist helped me so much.

And I got my daughter back.

She moved back in with me.

And frankly, I didn't have to do much until he started hurting her again.

Because whenever he saw that our bond was too strong to come between us,

Whenever he saw that he could not use her again, that he could not annihilate her from me,

He started showing his face again.

And started abusing her again—emotionally—until she understood what she had been through.

With the emotional support from Child Protective Services—which I was very disappointed with—but the social worker assigned to my daughter was great,

And my private therapist, whom I was paying for, was great.

With a lot of hard work, my daughter saw who her father was.

He started getting very angry at her again.

Whenever he saw that she was not playing along,

He just totally gave up on her.

He shut all contact with her.

And now, she—with the support of her social worker—blocked him.

She's not willing to give him another chance.

She's done with him.

She saw him for who he was.

Our bond is stronger than ever.

I think that now that Child Protective Services is involved, although it's not pleasant for me to have them in my life and have checkups all the time,

I feel more protected because we have our son as well.

And I'm really scared that after attempting to hurt me through our daughter,

He's going to try it with our son.

But now that CPS is involved, maybe it's going to be a little bit harder for him.

I think that—again—he tried to do something,

But he shot himself in the legs again.

Because Child Protective Services does not give a shit—not about me and not about him.

They give a shit about our kids.

And now that they watch him as well,

I think it's going to be harder for him to use our son against me.

So with all of this shit that happened, again, I can see the positive.

Like always, he tried to do something harmful,

And it backfired.

And now I am at ease.

I'm at peace.

I'm not scared of him anymore.

Chapter 28: Let Him Come

I know that if someone had taught me things that I know now about narcissism,

Maybe I wouldn't have let all of his actions and legal actions affect me mentally this way.

But I'm okay now.

Like—I don't give a shit about him.

I'm not scared anymore.

I was always scared thinking:

What if he files another lawsuit?

What if he goes to the police again?

What if he lies again?

What if, what if, what if?

Now I just don't give a shit.

Bring it on.

I can handle anything.

Like I handled him throughout the years,

I know that whatever he tries to do to me will backfire tenfold.

I keep moving on with my life.

I keep progressing.

I keep growing—at work, with my kids.

My bond with my daughter is the strongest now.

I keep thriving—whether it's financially or socially.

He just keeps going backward.

He's still led by so much poison and so much anger—it's unexplainable.

I think he lives in some kind of reality, and he believes it.

It's a sickness.

It's pathological lying.

It's making up a reality that doesn't exist and believing in it.

He's trying to get back at me for something I never did.

He's trying to make my life miserable.

This is his life's work.

Which is so pathetic.

Right now, I'm in a state in my life where I feel:

Why should I be afraid of him?

I used to feel so small.

Like he's this big monster that affects my life.

Now I understand that—

No.

He's the small one.

He's the one who's never going to do anything with his life.

He's stuck inside his anger.

He's stuck inside his control.

He's stuck inside his jealousy.

He can rot in hell, as far as I'm concerned.

And the whole point of this book?

It's because when I was researching narcissism,

I saw so many textbook descriptions.

Okay—they helped me understand what I was dealing with.

But I never read a true story.

From beginning to end.

That made me see I have nothing to be fearful of.

If I had known then what I know now,

I would have never let fear lead me.

This is the point of this book.

I'm pretty much sure I'll never be done with him 100% until our son is 18.

My daughter is now 16 and a half.

She's not in contact with him.

She blocked him.

She knows who he is.

She says she'll never get back in contact with him.

And I've just learned not to be afraid anymore.

I want people who go through the same hell as I did to know:

There is nothing to be afraid of.

You need to know that the truth is with you.

If you have everything documented—

Which survivors of narcissistic abuse usually do—

You have nothing to be afraid of.

And the most important thing:

Know this.

The narcissist thrives on your emotional reactions.

Do not—I repeat, do not—give it to them.

They will use it against you.

Whenever they push those buttons,

Whenever they try to do things to you—

Do. Not. React.

Go for a walk.

If it's possible at all, go no contact.

If you have kids with them, find a way to reduce contact to the bare minimum.

Like, I can give you an example.

Just a few days ago, he ruined my son's shoes that I bought.

They were his only pair.

It was the weekend. I couldn't buy new ones anywhere.

I asked him to replace them.

He ruined them—so he should replace them, right?

And he said:

"I'm not replacing anything. I'm not buying anything. Money comes to you easily. But to me? It's not coming easily."

Do you see how delusional these people are?

Do you understand that this person got an inheritance?

He got a free house.

He got a shitload of money.

He lived with his parents until he was 41 years old.

He never paid a bill in his life until he was 41.

Except for the little things, he paid and made me pay him back.

He never had any expenses.

I worked tooth and nail to get where I am today.

I work 12 hours a day.

I rip my ass off at work.

And money comes easily to me?

The person who has never had help in her life?

Who built everything with her own two bare hands?

This is pathetic.

These are exactly the tactics they will use to get you to respond.

And he sees that he has no control over me anymore.

So I can see his pathetic little ways—

He's trying to jab a little more. A little deeper.

Like with this phrase:

"Money comes easily to you."

He's looking to get this long text message,

Where I curse him.

Where I start defending myself.

Where he feels like a man—because he's not one.

He's just a pathetic little creature.

But know this:

This is their fuel.

Don't give it to them.

This is their food.

Starve them.

I will never, ever let him do anything to me again.

To me, he's dead.

He doesn't exist.

There is no reason for me to be in contact with him anymore.

And if he wants to sue me again, let him.

I will eat him without salt.

Let him try anything again.

I am not afraid.

And neither should you be.

THIS IS NOT THE END

IT'S THE BEGINNING

Printed in Dunstable, United Kingdom